Published in paperback in 2017 by Wayland

Wayland, an imprint of Hachette Children's Group
Part of Hodder & Stoughton
Carmelite House
50 Victoria Embankment
London EC4Y 0DZ

10 9 8 7 6 5 4 3 2 1

Editor: Debbie Foy
Design: Rocket Design (East Anglia) Ltd
Illustration: Alan Irvine

British Library Cataloguing in Publication Data
Harrison, Paul, 1969-
Science. -- (Truth or busted)
1. Science--Miscellanea--Juvenile literature.
2. Common fallacies--Juvenile literature.
I. Title II. Series
502-dc23

ISBN: 978 0 7502 7914 7

Printed and bound by CPI Group (UK) Ltd, Croydon, CR0 4YY

Wayland is a division of Hachette Children's Group,
an Hachette UK company
www.hachette.co.uk

All illustrations by Shutterstock, except 4, 11, 37, 47, 64, 65 and 90-91

EVERYTHING YOU THINK YOU KNOW ABOUT SCIENCE MIGHT BE WRONG...

read on!

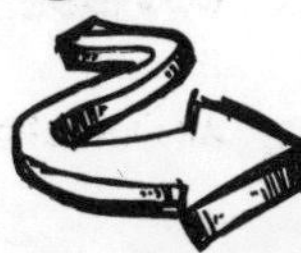

EVERYTHING?

Yes, perhaps. You'd be surprised by how many things you take as fact that are, in fact, utter baloney. But how can this be?

Often it's because scientists make new discoveries that change the way we think about something. Other times it's because we believe something because we've always believed it and believing something else just doesn't feel right. And sometimes we just get things wrong (don't worry about this too much though – as you'll soon discover, even the best scientists get stuff wrong).

Science is all about testing and retesting your ideas and **TRUTH OR BUSTED** *Human Beings Can Go Pop in Space* is your chance to test yourself to see how much you know about science. Do you believe the sky is blue? Or that chicken soup can cure a cold? Have you always thought that birds sitting on telephone wires are immune to electricity? Or that a sneeze is more deadly than a bullet? Can you spot which statements are TRUE and which ones are BUSTED?

On top of that you'll also find inside which movies were a big hit at the box office but were a big fail at science; the world's weirdest weather; and the scientists that paid the ultimate price for their work.

So read on – there's a whole world of information to discover inside.

'There's one born every minute,' they say, to describe suckers who'll believe nearly anything. Armed with a copy of this book, at least that sucker won't be you!

So you might hear myths like...

Look at the sky on a lovely sunny day. There isn't a cloud above you and the sky is a bright blue. It's what you would see and what I would see. Except what we see might not actually be the truth of the matter.

And the truth is...

Sunlight is in fact white. More remarkable still, this white light is actually the combination of lots of different colours: red, orange, yellow, green, blue, indigo and violet. This is called the spectrum and you see it every time you look at a rainbow – but what you are actually seeing is the light getting split up by water vapour.

The reason the sky looks blue is down to what's in the air. Our atmosphere is full of dust, gases and water vapour. All these different particles can scatter light – but blue light in particular. Of all the different colours it's the blue light that gets bounced around the most, and this is what we see when we look at the sky – bouncing blue light.

Verdict: **BUSTED**

If you sneeze with your eyes open they will pop out

A sneeze is a reaction to the nose being irritated and can help get rid of bacteria and germs. Sneezes can be pretty powerful, too – air gets pushed from your lungs and through your nose at up to 160 km/h (100 mph). That's a lot of force being generated and some people believe that this is why we close our eyes at the same time as we sneeze – because if we didn't our eyes would simply come flying out!

And the truth is...

Closing our eyes is simply a reaction and no one knows why we do it. There are plenty of people who can keep their eyes open when they sneeze and they aren't wandering about with their eyes hanging out. Give it a try yourself and see.

Verdict: BUSTED

A black hole in our galaxy will eventually suck in the Earth

Black holes are mysterious, powerful and, frankly, very, very scary. They are often the remains of stars that have died. When a large star dies it erupts in a massive explosion called a supernova. However, occasionally instead of exploding, the centre of some massive stars implode – shrink down to a tiny point. These remains can have the gravitational pull of hundreds of Suns.

The largest black holes are called supermassive black holes and have the gravity of millions of Sun-sized stars. Nothing can escape the pull of a black hole – even light itself. And the bad news is that scientists believe that there is a supermassive black hole at the centre of every galaxy – including our own.

Our galaxy is called the Milky Way and the supermassive black hole at its centre is called Sagittarius A. Scientists think that it has the same gravitational pull as 4 million Suns. Any nearby objects might well be sucked in – and add to the power of the black hole.

And the truth is...

The good news is that the Earth is probably too far away to get sucked in. The bad news is that there might well be a black hole scientists haven't spotted yet that is much closer. But the good news is that even if there is a closer one it still might not get us. But the bad news is the reason it won't get us is that in about 5 billion years scientists believe that the Sun will die and the Earth will be toast.

Verdict: **BUSTED**

Dinosaur Disasters

Even the biggest blockbusters get things horribly wrong. Take the *Jurassic Park* films for instance. They have fantastic computer generated images – but the science is a bit dodgy and an example of this is how the dinosaurs came to be alive today. A scientist was meant to have re-grown the dinosaurs from flies trapped in amber. The flies had bitten dinosaurs before they died and as a result had traces of dinosaur DNA inside them. DNA is like the code to what makes you unique. So the scientist took the DNA and grew dinosaurs from them.

This is wonky science because amber is great for preserving DNA – but not for millions and millions of years. Secondly the dinosaur DNA would have been mixed up with fly DNA so you wouldn't be able to separate the two strands.

Verdict = extinct idea!

Chopping onions can make you weep

Sad films, miserable music, and dead pets are all pretty much guaranteed to make you weep – but a root vegetable?

And the truth is...

The truth is that onions are more likely to bring tears to your eyes than slamming your head in a door. The reason lies in an evil mixture of chemicals inside the onion skin called amino acids and sulphurs. These are OK – unless you cut the onion. Then a fine gas with the tongue-tyingly long name of syn-Propanethial-S-oxide is transported through the air and into your eyes – promptly causing you to cry.

Avoid onion tears by wearing swim goggles near chopped onions. You will look like a wally, but at least you'll have dry eyes.

Verdict:

Air doesn't weigh anything

Sometimes things are described as being 'as light as air' meaning they have practically no weight at all. After all we are surrounded by air and we can't feel it weighing down on us. Look at a set of weighing scales – they won't show any weight from the air above it. So air can't weigh anything, right?

100% AIR

And the truth is...

Air weighs an awful lot. If you draw a square one metre by one metre on the ground the air above the square actually weighs around 9,000 kg (8.9 tons) – that's around 11 elephants' worth. The higher you go above sea level, the less the air will weigh because there will be less of it above you.

For life to flourish on this planet it has to adapt to the weight of the air above it. If we weren't designed to cope with the weight we'd be as flat as pancakes. The fact that we don't feel the weight is because we're used to it and are built to withstand it.

Verdict: BUSTED

There is more caffeine in tea than coffee

Tea and coffee both contain a substance called caffeine. This substance acts as a stimulant – it gives you a boost of energy. It's so effective a stimulant that athletes were banned from using it before competitions. However, too much caffeine is bad for you and can leave you feeling jittery, stressed and might stop you from sleeping. In very extreme cases it could kill you.

And the truth is...

Caffeine is present in many drinks and foods like chocolate. However the largest amounts are in tea and coffee. The amount varies depending on which type of tea or coffee you choose, but generally a cup of coffee has more caffeine than a cup of tea. Interestingly though, a portion of tea leaves has more caffeine than a portion of coffee grains – when boiling water is added to the leaves it reduces the amount of caffeine.

Verdict: TRUTH and BUSTED

but mainly busted

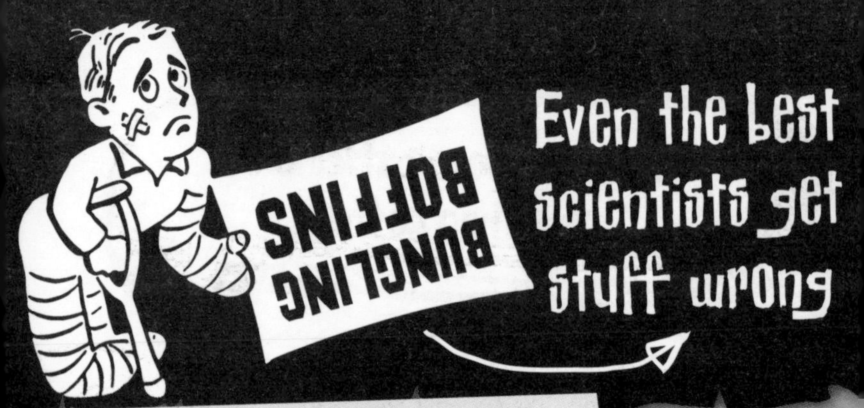

Charles Darwin

Darwin is known for his theory of evolution – how animals change over time and how and why new species arrive and old ones disappear. His ideas were revolutionary for their time and he is regarded as one of Britain's greatest scientists. But for a man who studied exotic animals, he certainly seems to have loved them. Loved the taste that is.

When Darwin was at Cambridge University he formed the Gourmet Club in which he and his fellow diners would eat exotic meat that you normally wouldn't be served at a restaurant. So he ate birds such as hawks, bitterns and even an owl.

This 'eat anything' approach came unstuck when Darwin travelled the world finding new species to send back to the UK to be studied. It was only at the end of a particularly fine meal that he realised he had just eaten a Lesser Rhea – a very rare bird he had spent weeks trying to find in South America. It was his only specimen.

Chicken soup can cure colds

The idea that chicken soup can cure colds has its roots far back in history. The Ancient Greeks made something similar to chicken soup as a cure for colds as did the Chinese. Chicken soup was also a traditional Jewish remedy and may have been used as a cold cure in Europe as early as the 12th century.

Chicken soup certainly has a lot of good things going for it, apart from the lovely taste. It is warm, which helps to unblock the passages; it also contains zinc and carnosine which are useful when treating colds as they help support your body's immune system. So chicken soup must be a cold cure – all those Greek, Chinese and Jewish people can't be wrong, can they?

And the truth is...

Yes they can. The zinc and carnosine in chicken soup won't make much difference to a cold – but at least it tastes good.

Verdict: **BUSTED**

Mount Everest is getting bigger

Mountains look like they've been around since the beginning of time; but the simple fact is that they haven't and the reason why lies in the way the Earth's surface is made. The surface isn't one solid piece; it's actually made up of big pieces like a massive jigsaw. These pieces are called plates, and the plates move about. They don't move very quickly – just a few centimetres a year – but over millions of years the world looks very different now to how it used to.

Another result of the plates moving is that mountains are made. Often when two plates meet, one plate slides underneath the other; but sometimes they hit and they crunch up a bit. The ripples become mountain ranges.

And the truth is...

Mount Everest is part of the Himalayan mountain range, which was formed when two plates crunched into each other. They're still crashing into each other today and as a result Mount Everest is growing at around 6cm (2 in) per year.

Raining Cats and Dogs

You might well have heard the expression 'it's raining cats and dogs', which generally means that it's pouring down. But did you know that sometimes it's not just rain or snow that falls from the skies?

For instance 'showers' of frogs have been recorded throughout history. And it's not just frogs that have taken to pretending to be rain. There have also been instances of fish, tomatoes, squid, coal, apples and worms dropping from the clouds.

Scientists call these 'non-aqueous showers' which basically means stuff that isn't rain falling from the sky. Although they have got a fancy name for it, they don't have an exact explanation for why it happens. Their best guess is that it's due to a mini whirlwind or waterspout that plucks something, a shoal of fish from the water for example, and dumps it inland.

Whatever the reason, next time you see clouds just hope it doesn't start raining cats and dogs!

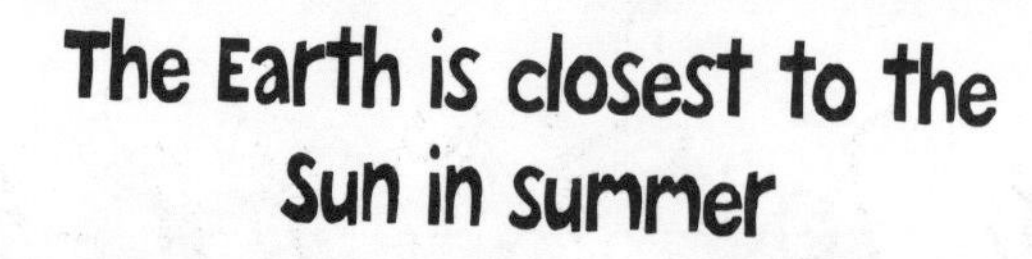

The Earth is closest to the Sun in summer

It's easy to forget that our lovely planet, Earth, is really just a rock spinning through space. It's not just hurtling in any random direction of course, it goes round and round our star, the Sun, taking a year to complete each trip round. And it's thanks to the Sun that we get all our natural heat and light.

The path we take around the Sun isn't a true circle; instead it's an ellipse, which is a bit like an oval. This means that the distance Earth is from the Sun varies – sometimes it's nearer and sometimes it's further away. It makes sense then, that when we are closer to the Sun we have summer and when we are further away we have winter.

And the truth is...

When the northern hemisphere (the bit we think of as being above the equator) has its summer it's actually at its furthest from the Sun. How? The answer is down to the fact that the Earth is on the wonk; it doesn't sit straight, in fact it leans over by 23°. This means as the Earth travels round the Sun one half of the world leans closer for one half of the year and then the other half leans closer for the second half. The half that leans closer has summer. If the Earth was straight, both the northern and southern hemispheres would have summer at the same time.

Verdict: BUSTED

KILLER SCIENCE

The scientists that died for their work - literally

If you've ever had an x-ray taken then remember to thank a remarkable woman from Warsaw, Poland, whose dangerous work still helps doctors today.

Marie Curie was born in Warsaw in 1867 and would become one of the most famous scientists of her generation. She won the Nobel Prize (awarded for great works in the field of the sciences, medicine, literature and peace) not just once, but twice.

She is most famous for her work with radioactive materials – in particular her pioneering research into x-rays. It was thanks to this work that x-ray machines were developed. It was also thanks to this work that she died. Marie Curie got leukaemia – cancer of the blood – caused by repeated exposure to radioactive materials. She died as a result of her illness in 1934, at the age of 66

Fatty foods are good for you

Eh? what? If you eat fatty foods you will get fat; or worse still suffer from a whole range of health problems such as heart disease. But there are lots of different sorts of fats, so try getting your mouth around these (er, ok... perhaps not all of them): saturated, monounsaturated, polyunsaturated, and trans fats. Are they all bad for us?

And the truth is...

The good news is that we need a certain amount of fat to survive. And that list of fats can be split into good fats and bad fats. Monounsaturated and polyunsaturated fats are generally good fats. They are found in things like salmon, or olive oil for example. So a diet that has these fats in is going to be good for you. Of course, as with all diet advice, don't eat too much of anything to be properly healthy. Too much good fat is bad for you too!

Deserts are always really, really hot

We all have a clear idea of what a desert looks like: hot, sandy, barren – a wilderness stretching for miles on end, frying under the relentless, burning sun. Deserts cover over one fifth of the land across the world and are actually home to a wide range of plants and animals. They have adapted to live in dry desert conditions; even in places like the Atacama desert which might not see rain for years and years at a time.

And the truth is...

The important word in the last paragraph was 'dry'. A desert is any place that receives less than 50 cm (19.6 in) of rainfall in a year. This might mean the type of desert described above, or cold dry regions. Antarctica, for example gets very little fresh rain or snow, so is actually classed as a desert.

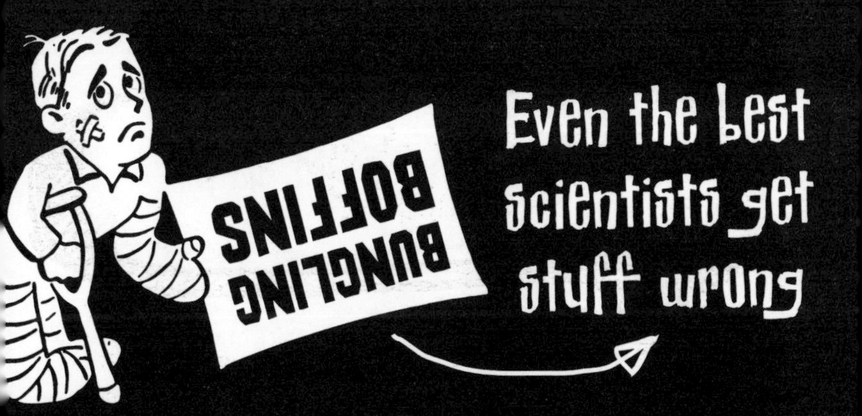

Sir Isaac Newton

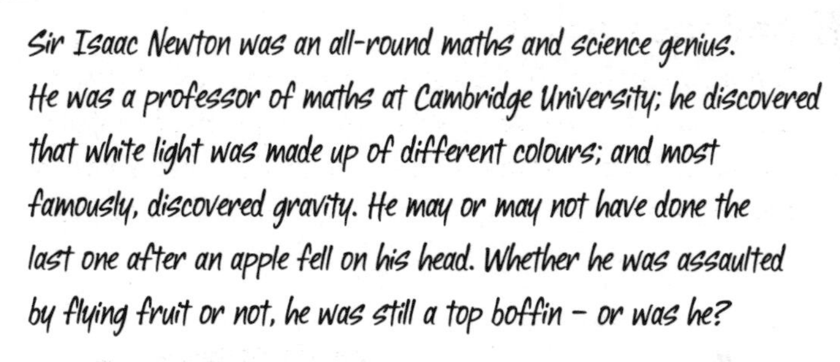

Sir Isaac Newton was an all-round maths and science genius. He was a professor of maths at Cambridge University; he discovered that white light was made up of different colours; and most famously, discovered gravity. He may or may not have done the last one after an apple fell on his head. Whether he was assaulted by flying fruit or not, he was still a top boffin – or was he?

He was famously grumpy and prone to bouts of depression. His ideas on gravity have been replaced by those of Albert Einstein. But the biggest slur on his good name as a scientist was his hobby of alchemy. This was the nonsensical idea that you could turn metals such as lead into gold or silver. But it was not only daft, it was also illegal!

Heat makes things get bigger

Take a big bar of metal – a nice thick one – and try stretching it. Grab one end in each hand and pull. Better still get someone else to pull one end while you pull the other. Nothing; it won't budge an inch. That's because iron is incredibly strong. However, if you apply heat to it, it'll get bigger – amazing, eh?

And the truth is...

Everything is made of atoms and atoms are on the move. We don't notice this because atoms are really, really tiny so the movement is really, really small. Heat makes the atoms move more, so the atoms need more space to move, so the object gets bigger. This can have quite a noticeable effect on big structures such as the Golden Gate Bridge in San Francisco, USA. Thanks to the summer heat it's nearly 1 metre (3 ft) longer than it is during the winter. Many structures have what they call expansion joints to absorb this growing and shrinking effect.

Star Flaws

Films set in space are known as science fiction and yet the science bits are rubbish. You could say that generally the science is purely erm... fiction. Take all those wonderful space ships for example, whooshing and zooming through space with those fantastic space ship noises. Except that's exactly the trouble – you can't hear anything in space (see page 36 to find out why), so spaceships just wouldn't make those noises.

Or take those ray guns, shooting those colourful laser beams with some devastating results. Except that's not how lasers work – for a start they don't come in all those great colours. In real life you can't see them. So you can't dodge out of the way of them. Lasers move at the speed of light – which is the fastest anything can move – so no matter how quickly you duck it won't be fast enough.

And don't get us started on lightsabers.

Human beings go pop in space

Human beings need a few things to survive: food, water and air being the basics. The most immediately important of the three is air and unfortunately for us, this can't be found in space (food and water are pretty scarce too). Space is near enough a vacuum, which means there is nothing there, no gas, no matter, nada, zilch, nothing. This has led people to suppose that because there is air pressure inside your body, it would make the body swell like a balloon and explode.

And the truth is...

The fact that our body is wrapped in skin stops us from exploding – our skin is strong enough to deal with the pressure. So although everything on your inside might want to get to the outside your skin keeps it all where it should be. After a few seconds in space without the correct gear you would pass out from lack of oxygen and eventually die – but you wouldn't explode.

Verdict: BUSTED

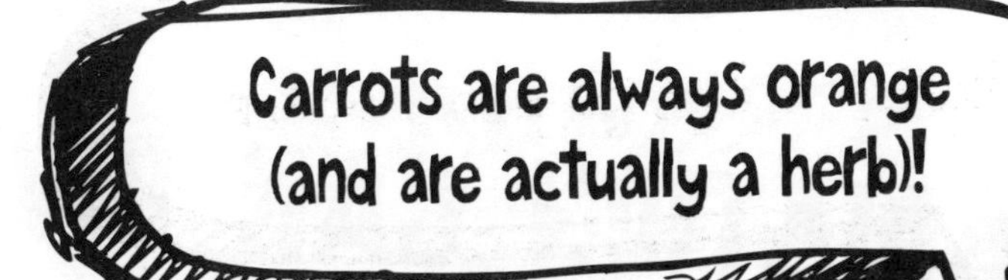

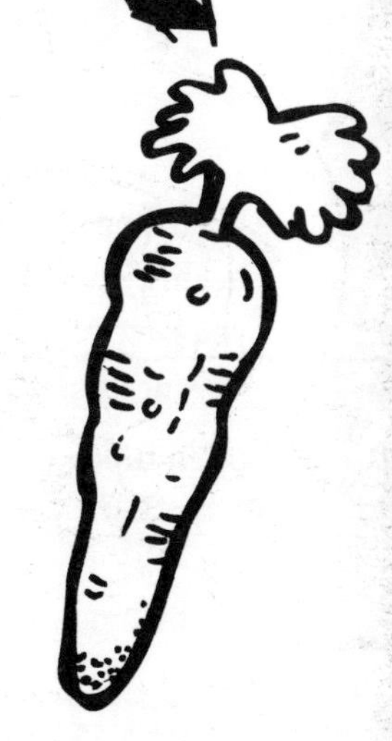

Carrots are one of the most popular vegetables in the world. We say that carrots are a root vegetable, which means we eat the part of the plant that grows underground. However carrots are actually part of the parsley family and therefore are technically a herb. Carrots are also a great source of vitamins and nutrients as well as having that wonderful orange colour.

And the truth is...

Carrots come in all sorts of colours: red, yellow, purple, and even white. It is believed that they were originally purple and have been bred to come in different colours. Orange carrots started to become popular in the 1400s. Some people think they were grown to celebrate William of Orange, the Dutch, and then English king, but there's not much evidence for this.

RADIATION CAN GIVE YOU SUPERPOWERS

It must be great being a superhero; you could fly, or have laser beam eyes, or the strength of fifty men. The only downside is you have to wear a silly costume with your underpants on top of your trousers. But how do you get to be a superhero?

Often superheroes get their super-skills in some surprising ways. See if you can match these superheroes to the method they got their powers.

SUPERHEROES

- ***Spiderman***
- ***The Hulk***
- ***The Fantastic Four***
- ***Daredevil***
- ***Captain America***

METHOD

- ***Gamma rays from an experiment that went wrong***
- ***Drinks a special formula and is exposed to 'vita-rays'***
- ***Bitten by radioactive spider***
- ***Exposed to radioactive material as a child***
- ***Flew through a cloud of cosmic radiation***

Answers:
Spiderman got bitten by a radioactive spider; the Hulk got his strength when he was exposed to too much radiation in an experiment that went wrong; the Fantastic Four flew through the cloud; Daredevil was exposed to radioactive material as a child and Captain America drank the formula and had the 'vita-rays'.

They all became superheroes, so radiation must be the answer!

And the truth is...

We are exposed to radiation all the time, but in very low doses so we don't notice. Radiation comes from the ground and from space; it even comes from mobile phones. Coming into contact with a large dose of radiation *would* have an effect – it would probably kill you. At the very least it would give you radiation sickness and a whole host of unpleasant symptoms such as vomiting, diarrhoea, gum disease and hair loss.

There's a good reason that superheroes only exist in comic books – in real life they'd be dead.

Verdict: ______ BUSTED

WEIRD WEATHER

Foam Storm

Think of all the different types of weather can you name:

Rain, Fog, Sleet, Hail, Sunshine, Drizzle, Mist, Snow, Foam...

Foam? That's right foam. In December 2011 residents of the coastal town of Cleveleys, UK, were hit by a storm that left drifts of white stuff covering streets and cars – and it was foam not snow. In places the foam was up to 1 metre (3 ft) deep. And it was the third time it had happened that year.

It appears that the foam had blown in from the sea by strong winds. At first no one was sure what the foam was made of and the worry was it was some kind of sea pollution. However it appears that the foam might well be the remains of microscopic sea creatures that can sometimes be brought together by the right wind and sea conditions. Whatever its cause, it's not the kind of foam you'd want to find in your bath, that's for sure.

Water goes down the plug hole in different directions north or south of the equator

The Earth rotates which is why we get night and day. However that is not the only effect this rotation has. It is also responsible for weather patterns which is due to something called the Coriolis effect. This is a complicated theory that concerns how objects move and it's often given as the reason why water spins down the plug hole in different directions north or south of the equator.

And the truth is...

The direction water spins as it goes down the plug hole has more to do with a whole range of different factors, such as: the way the sink is made, the direction the water was already moving before the plug is pulled, and how the plug is pulled. The Coriolis effect is way too small to have any noticeable effect.

Verdict: BUSTED

No two snowflakes are the same

Snowflakes are one of the most basic and yet most beautiful objects in the natural world. In essence they are just ice crystals that fall from the clouds. A snowflake might be a single ice crystal or a collection of many ice crystals. However, they all have one thing in common; no matter how many crystals they are formed of they are all hexagonal, because that is the shape ice crystals are. So if all snowflakes are hexagonal does that mean they are all the same?

And the truth is...

The exact shape of a snowflake depends on lots of differing factors; how moist the air is or how cold it is for example. This can have a big effect on the shape. Each crystal will be hexagonal, but the variety within that basic outline can be staggering. There can be flakes with six long needle-like arms; or very flowery looking arms for instance. In fact the possibilities are literally endless – so no two snowflakes are ever exactly the same.

Verdict: ____________________

In space nobody can hear you scream

Sound is amazing. It can travel huge distances and amazing speeds, but sometimes you won't hear even the loudest noises. For example, elephants make a sound that can travel for miles, but this is nothing compared to the noises whales make. These whale songs can travel hundreds of kilometres – but we don't hear them because whales and elephants make sounds we can't hear. But a scream we can hear, so surely we should be able to hear one in the quiet of deep space.

And the truth is...

Sound travels at around 1,225 km/h (761 mph) through the air. But even more astounding is the fact that it travels four times quicker through water than through air. That's because sound needs molecules to travel. The molecules vibrate against each other and that's how noise moves. The molecules are closer together in water than in air, so sound goes faster. However in space there are no molecules so sound doesn't travel at all. And no travel means no noise – you can scream as loud as you want, but nobody is going to hear you.

Verdict:

A sneeze is more deadly than a bullet

A bullet is an effective way of killing or injuring someone. It needs a charge of exploding gunpowder to provide the force to send it flying through the air. If it hits someone, things get very messy indeed. A sneeze on the other hand is a reaction to something irritating your nose. It's easy to see which one is more dangerous.

And the truth is...

Perhaps it's not quite so clear after all. A sneeze is also a very effective way of spreading germs, and germs can be exceedingly dangerous. In 1918 World War I finished claiming the lives of up to 17 million people. The same year there was an outbreak of Spanish flu. It spread across much of the world killing an estimated 50 million people. So the flu killed more than a world war – better get your tissues ready.

KILLER SCIENCE

The scientists that died for their work – literally

Sylvester H Roper (1823–96)

It might seem a bit odd these days, but during the early development of cars and motorbikes nobody could decide what would be the best way to power these vehicles. For a number of years steam-power was very popular – in fact in 1906 the fastest car on the planet was powered by steam.

One of the early pioneers of steam-powered vehicles in the United States was Sylvester H Roper. He built his first steam-powered bike in 1869 – a noisy, smoky machine that scared horses. Around the same time he also built a steam-powered carriage. It looked like something a horse would pull, but with a steam engine instead of the horse.

Motorbikes seemed to have been Roper's real passion though. In 1896 he developed a bike that was too quick for racing cyclists to keep up with when he displayed it on a cycle track in Boston. Convinced he could get more speed from his machine, Roper pushed his motorbike to its limits – and promptly crashed it. Roper did not survive.

WEIRD WEATHER

Summer Snow

There are some things you just expect from the weather. It should be sunny and warm in the summer and the winter should be cold and wet, with a good chance of snow. However it appears that occasionally somebody has forgotten to remind the weather of these basic rules.

Summer snowfall occurs across the globe at seemingly random moments – often when other parts of the country are baking in the summer heat. In July 2011 snow blocked a state highway in Sichuan, China. In 2010 snow fell in New South Wales, Australia one week after the same region had been experiencing 45°C (113°F) summer temperatures.

Such strange occurrences are sometimes due to a mix of unseasonal cold temperatures, wet weather and the height of the area experiencing the snow. Nevertheless, it's still a surprise if you're still wearing shorts and a t-shirt.

One side of the Moon is permanently dark

You hear expressions like 'moonshine' and it makes it sound like the Moon provides its own light, like the Sun. It doesn't – we see the Moon because it is lit up by the Sun. But what do we see?

If you look at the Moon you always see the same side. The Moon might wax and wane – go to a full then to a crescent shape – but it's always the same bit of it we see. We never get to see the other side. This has led many people to suggest that the Moon doesn't rotate and therefore there is a 'dark side' of the Moon that never gets lit up by the Sun.

And the truth is...

Those people are wrong on both counts. The Moon does rotate, it's just that its rotation roughly coincides with Earth's, so we always see the same face. Secondly, as the Moon orbits around the Sun, all of its faces see the light of the Sun. When we see the new Moon – when it looks like the Moon is barely there at all – is when the Moon is between us and the Sun. Then what we think of as the 'dark side' of the Moon is actually getting the Sun's light.

Verdict:

BUSTED

A baby can become a genius by listening to Mozart

In 1993 scientists made a surprising discovery. They found that by playing music by the famous Austrian composer Wolfgang Amadeus Mozart people performed better in mental tests than people who had listened to different music or none at all. The findings became known as 'the Mozart effect'. A similar trial was conducted on pre-school children, and they too seemed to perform better after exposure to Mozart. Logically, it made sense that playing music to both unborn and newborn babies would also be beneficial.

And the truth is...

'The Mozart effect' is very controversial. Some scientists have been unable to replicate the results. Also, the effect itself wears off after 12–15 minutes (though longer for children). Worse still, one of the scientists from the original experiment also suggested later that there was no evidence that it would make babies more intelligent. So you can put the Mozart CD away now Mum.

Verdict: BUSTED

Claudius Galen

Claudius Galen was an Ancient Greek surgeon who made his name working for the Romans. His first job was patching up gladiators, which gave him plenty of opportunity to see how the body was put together, thanks to the horrific injuries. It seems that Galen did such a good job, he was eventually hired as personal doctor to the Roman Emperor Marcus Aurelius.

Without a steady stream of injured gladiators to stick back together, Galen had more time on his hands. He studied the human body and how it works in more detail than anyone previously. His discoveries became the basis of medical knowledge for the next thousand years.

Unfortunately Galen got a number of things wrong. For example he thought the liver pumped blood around the body and that the heart was filled with air. Well – you can't get everything right, can you?

There is no gravity in space

Gravity is the force that keeps us on the ground and stops us from floating off into space. There's gravity on the Moon too; but as the Moon is only one sixth the size of the Earth its gravity is only as sixth as strong. That's why astronauts could bounce around the surface like they did.

And the truth is...

The further away from the Earth you get the weaker the pull of gravity is. So, astronauts in space can float around inside their spacecraft. However that doesn't mean there is no gravity there – on the contrary there's loads of it. For example it's the Earth's gravity that keeps the Moon orbiting around us. It's the Sun's gravity that keeps all the planets orbiting around it. Without it we could be literally anywhere.

Verdict: BUSTED

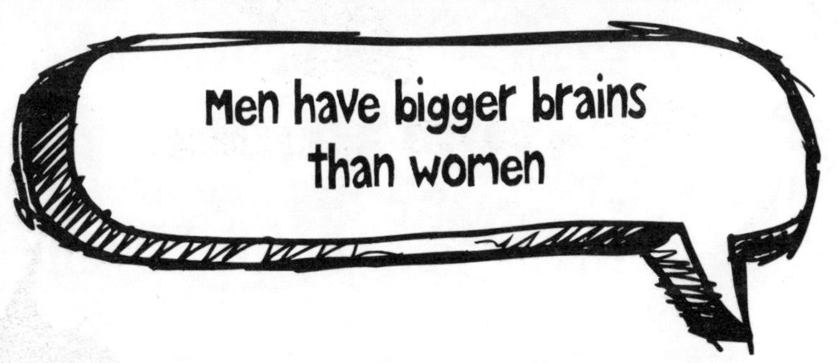

Men have bigger brains than women

Who's better – boys or girls? It's an argument that's been going for years and years and years; and will keep going as long as there are still boys and girls on the planet. One of the big arguments is who is more intelligent – who's got the biggest brains?

Studies show that when babies are born, baby boys tend to have bigger brains. However they also tend to be bigger overall – girls born the same size have exactly the same size brain. Yet as we grow up men's brains tend to be around 10% bigger than women's. But does this mean men are more intelligent? No, as studies also show that men simply have bigger heads. Besides, it's not how big your brain that matters – it's how you use it that counts.

Verdict:

but so what?

Aristotle

Aristotle was an Ancient Greek and all round super-brain. He studied biology, physics, mathematics and philosophy and was one of the greatest thinkers of all time.

Aristotle was the first person to try grouping animals into families and species. His system is very similar to one still used today. He believed in studying and experimenting and had a very scientific and logical way of thinking about issues.

But he did get a lot of things wrong. He thought earthquakes were caused by underground winds, for example; and that the Universe had no beginning and would never end. Some of the things he got wrong you would have thought would have been easy to check up on. For example he thought women had fewer teeth than men, and that flies had four legs.

So Aristotle proves that no matter how bright you are, you're going to get something wrong sooner or later.

Barbie dolls are based on a real person

For over 50 years the Barbie doll has been a worldwide bestseller. In 1959 its inventor, Ruth Handler, watched her daughter, Barbara, dressing up some paper dolls. She realised that a plastic version would be better so she came up with the idea for Barbie.

And the truth is...

Barbie may be named after a real person, but that's where any connection with reality ends. The proportions of the doll are nothing like those of a real woman. Her legs and neck are too long, her waist is too thin and her feet are too small.

Humans also have a large, heavy head. This makes balancing a tricky act to master and is one of the reasons why toddlers fall over so often. If a real person was shaped like a Barbie doll with those tiny feet and massive head they'd spend most of their time falling over!

Sitting too close to the TV is bad for your eyes

How many times have you been told that you shouldn't sit too close to the television? It'll ruin your eyesight. You'll get square eyes. You'll turn into a lazy, bloated, couch potato. It's been the same message since television first started to become popular in the 1950s.

And the truth is...

Televisions produce radiation – and too much radiation can be bad for you. Back in the 1950s no one really understood how harmful the radiation coming from televisions could be and watching too much TV caused some people eye problems such as myopia, or short-sightedness as it is more commonly known. Nowadays televisions shield viewers from radiation, so sitting too close won't harm you. Mind you, watch too much television and you might get eye-strain; and you'll definitely turn into a couch potato.

Verdict: Mainly **BUSTED**

Time Travelling Travesties

The idea of time travel has interested scientists and movie-makers alike, but thinking about it and how it would really work makes your head hurt.

1. **The present as you know it wouldn't exist.** Any changes in the past would alter the chain of events that led to everything being where it was in the future.
2. **An alternate Universe would be formed alongside the original.** The alternate Universe would be like the original Universe, but changed from the moment the time travellers arrived.

In the *Back to the Future* films (where a scientist makes a time machine from an old sports car) both of these things happen, which it can't as it's either one or the other. But the biggest problem with time travel into the past is that it's not possible. You would have to travel faster than light to do so, and top scientist Einstein tells us that nothing travels faster than light – not even an old sports car or a Tardis.

A tomato is really a fruit

We all know the difference between fruit and vegetables. Fruit is the healthy stuff you can eat for snacks and/or dessert. Vegetables are the healthy things that come on your plate next to the meat or fish. Or if you're a vegetarian it's the stuff that comes on your plate. And if you're a vegetarian you should really know the difference. And just to prove to yourself that you know which is which take this simple quiz:

Decide whether the following foods are either fruits or vegetables:

(a) Tomato

(b) Orange

(c) Cabbage

(d) Onion

(e) Pumpkin

(f) Turnip

(g) Leek

(h) Apple

(i) Banana

(j) Potato

(k) Peas

(l) Sweetcorn

(m) Radish

(n) Red pepper

(o) Cucumber

Answers

Fruit: a, b, e, h, i, k, l, n, o **Vegetables:** c, d, f, g, j, m

A simple way of telling the difference between the two is that fruit have seeds and vegetables don't. Peas and sweetcorn are actually seeds, and that's why they are fruit. This also means that nuts technically are fruit; as are cereals like wheat and other grains.

Of course how we use these various fruits and vegetables is what is really important. As the famous quote puts it:

'Knowledge is knowing a tomato is a fruit; wisdom is knowing not to put it in a fruit salad.'

We don't know who said it, but they got it spot on.

And the truth is...

Surprisingly a tomato is a fruit, and so are many things you might have thought were vegetables. Have a look at the answers to the quiz and see.

Verdict:

St Elmo's Fire

You would think that if a sailor saw the mast of their ship on fire they would be worried. However that's not always the case. Since ancient times sailors have occasionally seen the ends of their masts glowing with what looked like a strange unearthly fire that would leave no damage. Sailors took the appearance to be good luck and called it St Elmo's fire after the patron saint of sailors, St Elmo.

What they were actually seeing was an electric spark, a bit like an open air neon sign. It was a result of there being a lot of electricity in the atmosphere, like when a thunderstorm was in the area.

It's not just ships that are affected, tall spires can also be seen to glow in the same way. Usually St Elmo's fire appears as a thunderstorm moves away – so maybe those sailors were right after all when they thought it was good luck.

Your IQ – or Intelligence Quotient to give it its full name – is a rough measure of your intelligence. Scientists measure your IQ by taking your mental age (which they get from a series of tests) and dividing it by your actual age and then multiplying the number by 100. The final figure is your IQ – a score of 100 is said to be average.

Obviously people know a lot more when they are 20 years old as compared to when they were 5 years old, so obviously their IQ has gone up. Or has it?

And the truth is...

IQ tests are adjusted for age. After you reach 16 the idea of a 'mental age' is abandoned and instead your test results are compared to what is considered to be the average score for your age. So, although you might know more stuff your IQ score would stay roughly the same throughout your life.

Verdict:

Diamonds are made in volcanoes

According to a famous old song, diamonds are a girl's best friend. Now the girl's living, breathing, human best friend might take exception to that, but we can kind of see what the song is saying: diamonds are so precious and valuable anyone would want one.

Diamonds are basically just lumps of tightly pressed carbon, but when cut and polished are uniquely beautiful. Because of this diamonds have been prized throughout history and have often been used in jewellery, as they are today. One of the biggest diamonds ever found, named the Cullinan, can be found in the crown jewels of the British Royal Family.

Diamonds are also the hardest natural substance on Earth. It is used in industry for lots of different jobs, such as cutting other materials, or grinding substances down.

But how is such a useful substance made? Many people think diamonds can occur in coal seams, as coal is basically compressed carbon, too.

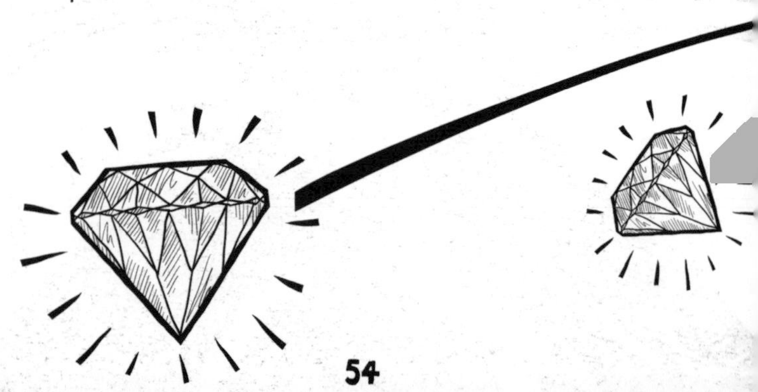

And the truth is...

Diamonds are much older than the first plants, and as coal is fossilized plant matter then that rules that idea out. For diamonds to form there needs to be extreme pressure and extreme heat – around 1050 °C (1922 °F) would do it – and the only place to find that combination is in the Earth's mantle, which lies below the Earth's surface layer.

And the only way for diamonds to get from the mantle to the surface is to hitch a ride on a volcanic eruption.

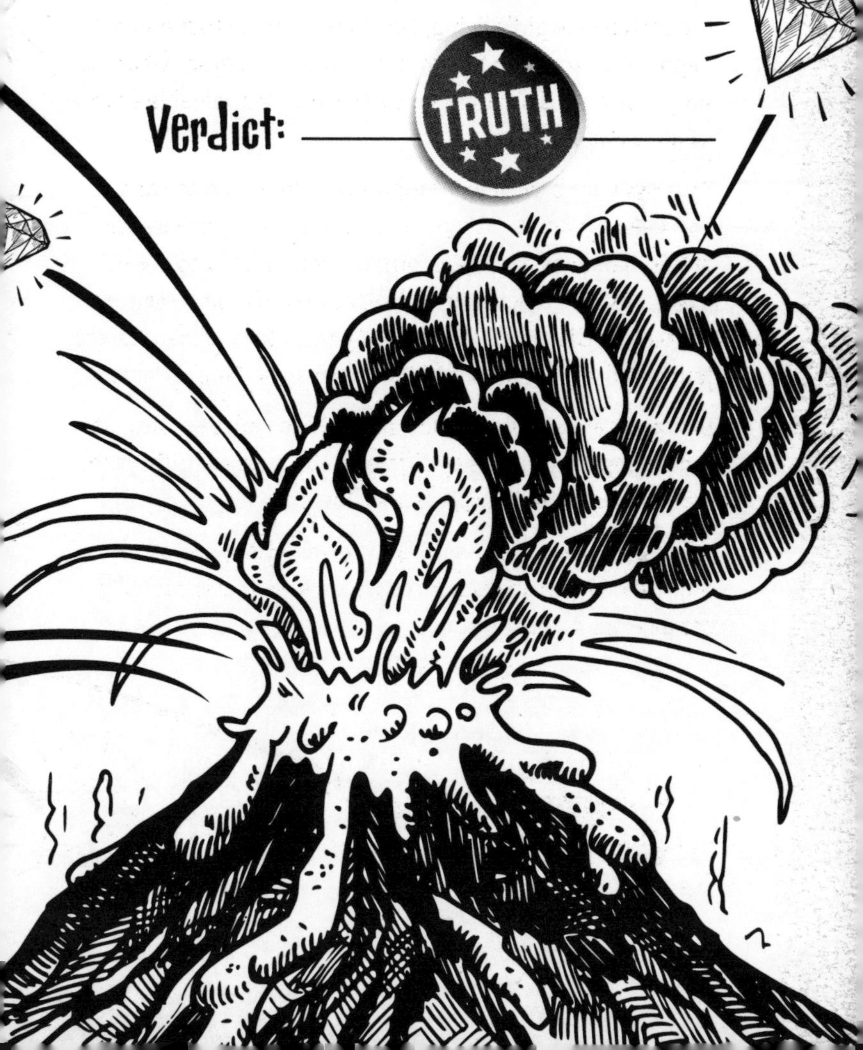

KILLER SCIENCE

The scientists that died for their work - literally

Jean François Pilâtre de Rozier

In France in 1783 the Montgolfier brothers launched the first unmanned hot-air balloon. Their ultimate aim was to launch a balloon with people on board. But who would fly it?

Step forward Jean François Pilâtre de Rozier; teacher, chemist and inventor. His short flight propelled him to fame and fuelled his desire to experiment more in the brave new world of balloons. It would prove to be a brief passion.

In 1785 Pilâtre de Rozier attempted to cross the English Channel in what would be only his third flight – this time in his own homemade balloon. This balloon used hot air and hydrogen, a lighter-than-air gas. Unfortunately hydrogen is also highly flammable. Pilâtre de Rozier's balloon exploded mid-air and he entered the history books as the world's first aircraft fatality.

Back from the Dead

Mary Shelley wrote *Frankenstein* in the early 1800s and it has been made into countless films. The story is of a mad scientist (scientists in films are always mad) called Dr Frankenstein who stitches together various bits of dead bodies and brings his creation to life using electricity.

Shelley might well have been inspired by the work of Luigi Galvani. This Italian scientist noticed that electricity made the legs of a dead frog move, concluding that electricity was a vital part of life. His experiments were groundbreaking.

They were also wrong. A modern-day defibrillator might get a heart working again, but it takes more than electricity for life. Even if Dr Frankenstein could have connected all the veins and arteries together, there would be too much decay, blood loss and tissue damage for his creation ever to live — never mind move.

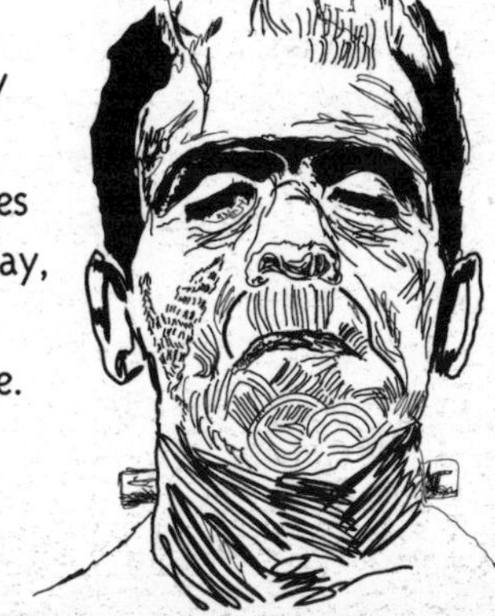

There is life on other planets

Are there aliens out there? Well, before we ask that question we've got to work out what we mean by alien life. Scientists would say that it means anything from little green men whizzing around in flying saucers to tiny bacteria, too small to see, clinging to a lump of asteroid. With such a big range of life to look for, is it really believable that we are all alone in this universe of ours? Surely at least one of those billions of stars must have a planet orbiting it with some kind of life on it.

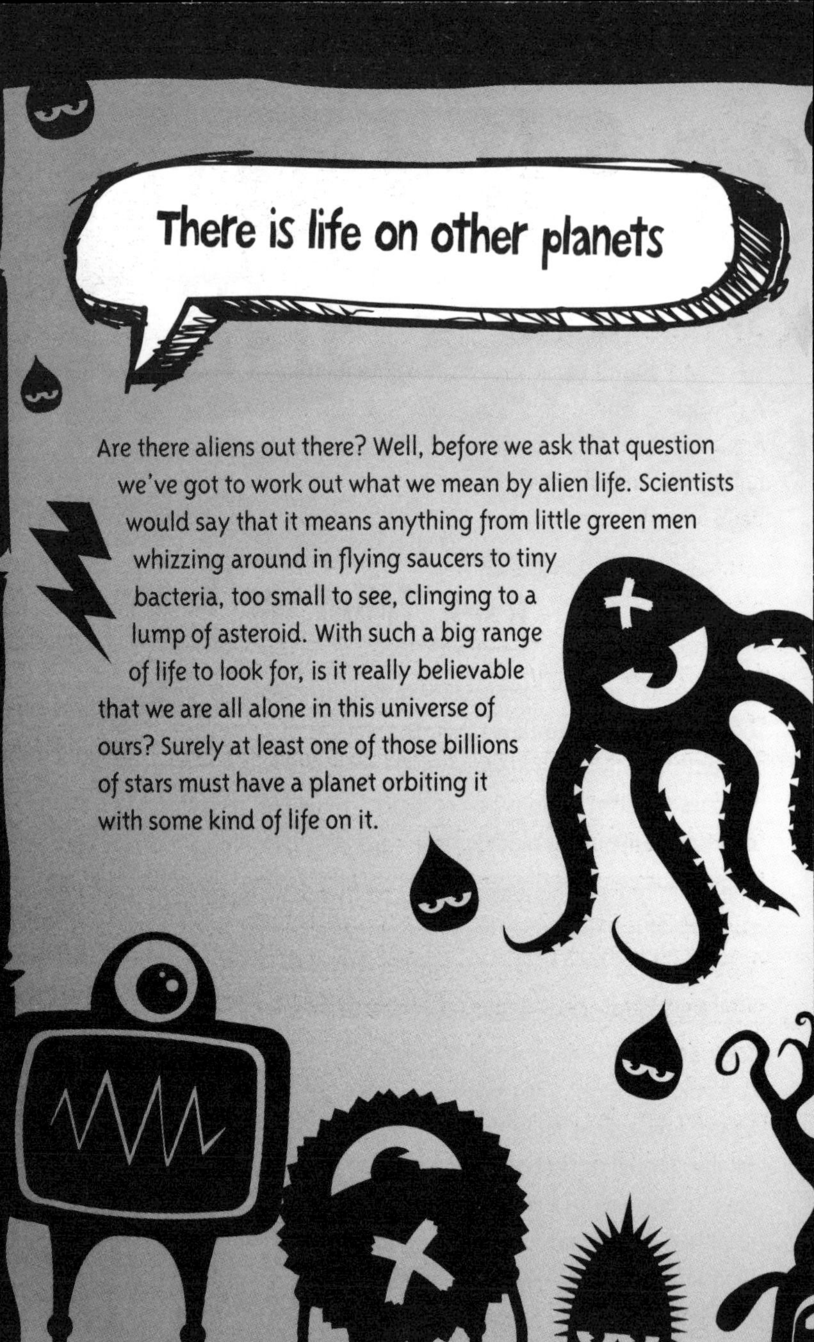

And the truth is...

We've not found anything yet, but scientists are still looking. A couple of years ago it looked as if life had been found. A meteorite that had landed on Earth had what looked like remains of ancient space bacteria – but that seems to have been a false alarm.

Instead scientists have been concentrating their search on planets roughly similar to Earth, orbiting at a similar kind of distance from a star as Earth does from the Sun. The reason for this is that many scientists believe that Earth has the perfect conditions for life as we know it. Earth has water and isn't too hot or too cold, which gives rise to the nickname for planets like Earth – 'Goldilocks planets'.

For many years the difficulty was finding planets like ours. Many planets are made of gas, like Jupiter, so don't have a proper surface. Others are in the wrong place. However, scientists now know of at least 54 planets similar to Earth.

Another interesting discovery was found here on Earth. A new form of bacteria was found that could live in conditions that we didn't think anything could live in before. This means there could be alien life out there in places where we haven't been looking. Watch this erm...space!

Verdict: 

for now

Swimmers shave their legs to go faster

Athletes who compete in many different types of sport shave their legs – both the women and the men. Most people think this is because the hair slows the athletes down. This seems logical enough – after all, have you ever seen a hairy racing car? Or think about the fastest animals – cheetahs, race horses, greyhounds. They don't exactly have big shaggy coats do they?

And the truth is...

Athletes shave for different reasons. Bodybuilders do it to look good. Cyclists do it in case they fall off their bikes – it makes patching their legs up easier. Swimmers do it because it makes a tiny difference to their speed as they travel through the water. Is it worth it? Well the difference between first and second in a swimming race is sometimes as little as one hundredth of a second, so the quick answer is yes!

Verdict: 

Meteorites are boiling hot when they hit the ground

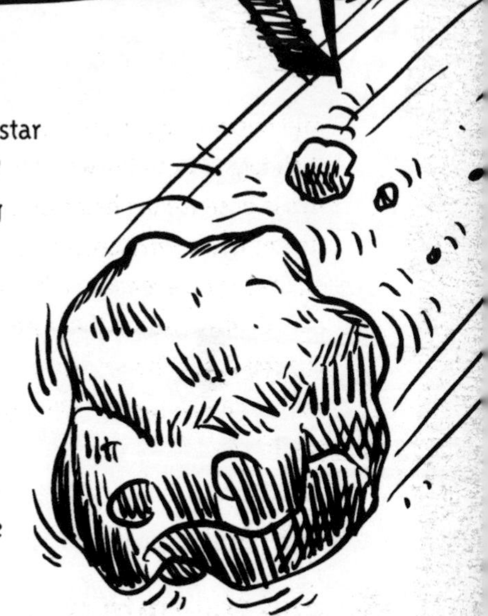

Have you ever seen a shooting star streaking across the night sky? In reality what you were seeing was probably a meteor – a piece of space rock burning up as it travels through the Earth's atmosphere. The heat is generated by the speed the meteor is travelling and the friction that is caused by the air. So, all that heat must make the rock hot, right?

And the truth is...

Space is really cold, so space rocks are really cold too. A quick blast through the Earth's atmosphere isn't enough to warm them right through. Also, the outside layer gets blasted off as it burns so by the time the meteor hits the ground – and becomes a meteorite, the name scientists call meteors on the ground – it should be cool.

Verdict: BUSTED

Edward Jenner

Jenner didn't really get anything wrong as such, it's more that his working practices would raise a few eyebrows today – in fact he would probably be arrested.

He is best known today for finding a cure for smallpox, which was a common disease before the 1800s and possibly the biggest killer of children at the time. However Jenner noticed that milk maids never seemed to get smallpox. They did catch a mild disease from cows occasionally, called cowpox, but this was not fatal. Jenner wondered if infecting someone with cowpox would stop them from getting smallpox.

Now here is where his actions would be seen as wrong today. To test his theory he injected an eight year old boy called James Phipps with cowpox. Then Jenner tried to give Phipps smallpox. Phipps did not get the disease (just as well really, or Jenner would be on a murder charge). Jenner tested his theory further by experimenting on himself and his own son. All survived and Jenner was famous.

Science can be very confusing at times. Take the Sun for example. Without it we would die out pretty quickly, which would be very bad news – for us anyway. So the Sun is a good thing. Ozone is found in our atmosphere and it blocks the Sun's rays. So ozone must be bad.

Wrong! The ozone blocks the harmful rays that come from the Sun, stopping us from dying out – which we've already decided would be a bad thing. So the Sun is bad (sometimes) and ozone is good.

And the truth is...

Ozone is bad for you. What? Yep ozone is bad for you. When it's high up in the atmosphere it's great; when it's low down near the ground it's a nightmare causing breathing problems that can kill you (which, as we know is a bad thing). So high ozone good, low ozone bad.

We told you science could be confusing!

You taste food with your nose

Your nose is really useful; it's particularly good at smelling stuff and as the place you can go snot mining for bogies. Your tongue is very useful too; in particular for tasting things and for sticking out at people you don't like. So there we have it: nose for smelling, tongue for tasting.

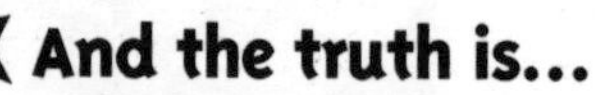

And the truth is...

Although you taste with your tongue, the tongue does a fairly basic job. It can tell the difference between sweet, sour, bitter, salty and umami (a kind of savoury taste) – and that's it. It's actually the nose's job to flesh out the tastes, by giving you the smell. Your nose can recognise thousands of different smells, and the brain uses this information along with the taste information to give you the full picture of what you're eating.

If you don't believe this then eat something when you have a blocked nose – your food won't taste half as good.

Verdict:

On a cold day the best advice is to wear a hat as you lose up to 45% of your body heat through your head. It's such good advice that the US army researched it and put it into one of their training manuals in 1970.

And the truth is...

The results of an experiment are only as good as the experiment itself. The army experiment involved dressing soldiers in Arctic gear and then making them really cold. The results showed that most heat was lost through the head – but that's because it was the only uncovered part of their bodies. If the soldiers had simply worn big furry hats and underpants, most body heat would have been lost from their torso, arms and legs.

Your head doesn't lose heat any faster than anywhere else – but it's still a good idea to wear a hat when it's cold.

Light travels at

How fast is fast? Running is faster than walking, for example, but racing cars are faster than running. Take the quiz below to see if you can work out who is faster.

Rank these in order of fastest to slowest:

Answers:

Peregrine falcon 320 km/hr (200 mph)
Cheetah 100 km/hr (65 mph)
Racehorse 60 km/hr (37 mph)
Olympic sprinter 37 km/h (23 mph)
Snail 0.42 km/h (0.26 mph)
Sloth 0.24 km/h (0.15 mph)

300,000 km/hr

So, although an Olympic sprinter might seem unbelievably quick to a sloth, the peregrine falcon puts them all in the shade. But what about light? It might seem odd to talk about the speed of light at all. You switch on a light switch, and the light is there immediately. Or is it?

Actually the light seems to be there straight away because light is travelling from the light bulb to your eyes unbelievably quickly – speeds that a falcon could only dream of travelling. But how fast is fast – 300,000 km/hr?

And the truth is...

Light travels much, much quicker than that – around 300,000 km per second. It is quite probable that nothing travels faster than light.

Although this means that light reaches you almost immediately from a light bulb, this is not true when you look at the huge distances between objects in space. For example, the Sun is around 150 million km (92 million miles) away from Earth. This means that the Sun's light takes roughly 8 minutes to reach the Earth. The light from distant stars can take months to get to Earth – imagine how long a sloth would take!

Verdict: BUSTED

Bacteria are good for you

'Have you washed your hands?'

'It's covered in germs!'

'Don't eat that, it's dirty!'

Ever heard this? It's pretty good advice, after all bacteria can be truly deadly. It's amazing to think that something so small – bacteria are made of just one, single cell – can be so harmful. But then, bacteria are amazing things. They are not plants and they are not animals, they are in a group all of their own. And their strength comes from numbers as bacteria multiply really quickly – the cells divide themselves into two, which then divide themselves and so on. Bacteria are like a constantly growing army of evil.

And the truth is...

There are plenty of different types of bacteria out there which can do you harm. Doctors call them pathogens. But without bacteria we'd be in a lot of trouble, too. Our intestines are full of them and without them we wouldn't be able to digest a lot of the things we eat. Good bacteria also help our immune systems to stay healthy. And some of the bacteria in our food make it taste the way it does. You couldn't make cheese and yogurt, for example, without bacteria.

So, some bacteria are bad, some are good and some are just downright tasty.

Your brain cells die off as you get older

Age does terrible things to the human body. Hair falls out from where you want it (your head, mainly) and grows where you don't want it (your nose and ears). Your skin gets wrinkly, your eyesight gets worse, your hearing gets worse, your reaction speeds slow down, and your joints ache. Worse still, from the age of 25 your brain cells start dying off. By the age of 80 it's amazing you can do anything or remember anything at all. Which might be why grown ups are always forgetting stuff!

★ And the truth is...

Scientists have discovered that although brain cells die off, people can also regenerate, or grow, new brain cells. The good news doesn't stop there. Once a person gets past middle age, the speed at which one brain cell works with another brain cell actually speeds up. So while the body slows down, the brain works quicker!

Verdict: ______

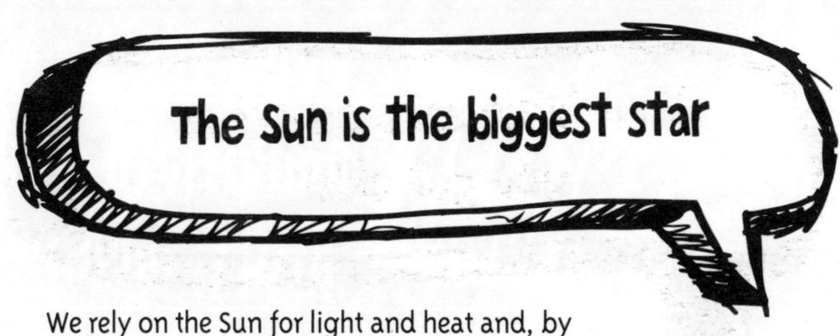

We rely on the Sun for light and heat and, by extension, life itself. It's our closest star, lying a mere 150 million km (93 million miles) away, which in space terms is a tiny distance. For example our next nearest star is Proxima Centauri which is around 399 trillion km (248 trillion miles) away. As the Sun is so close it looks much bigger than other stars, which look like small dots of light in the sky.

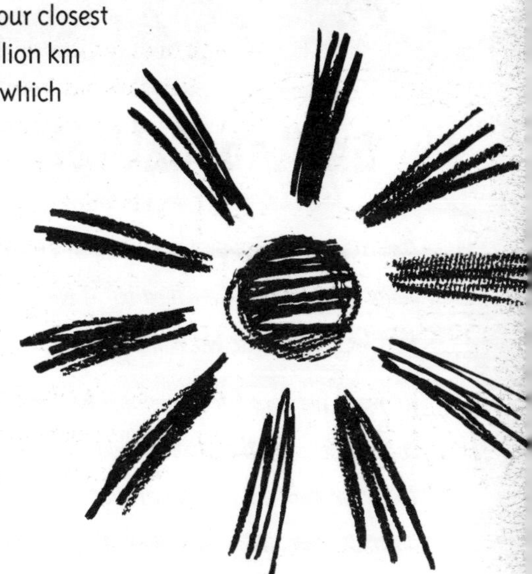

And the truth is...

Although all those stars look the same to the naked eye there are actually lots of different sizes. There are tiny dwarf stars, medium sized stars, giants and massive supergiants. The Sun is a run-of-the-mill, medium sized star – quite boring in star terms really. But it's our star and we love it.

Verdict: BUSTED

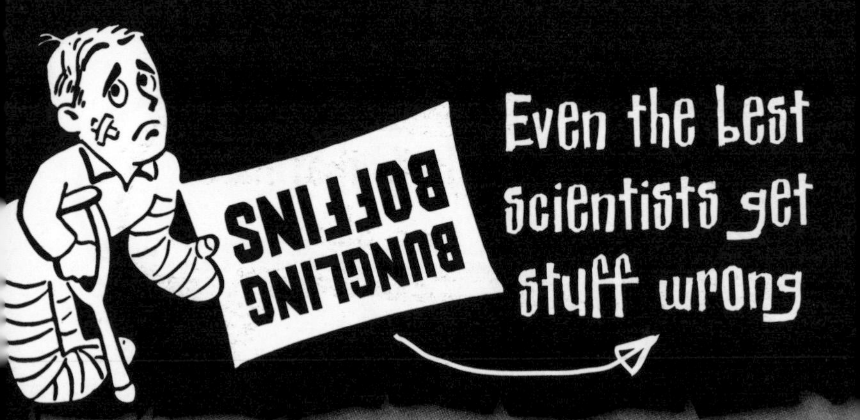

Galileo Galilei

Galileo was born near Pisa, Italy in 1564. He studied medicine, philosophy and mathematics but it was in the field of astronomy that he really made his name.

He made his own telescopes and he used them to make detailed observations of the Moon as well as other planets and moons in the solar system. He argued that the Sun was at the centre of the solar system, which was against the theory of the day that the Earth was at the centre of the Universe.

Galileo also used his telescope to study the Sun. This is a ridiculously dangerous thing to do and can easily blind you. Galileo went blind himself and many people claim that this was at least in part due to his experiments.

Why the idea came about that kings, queens, lords and ladies and the like have blue blood seems to be shrouded in mystery. Why should they be singled out anyway – we all have blue blood. Want proof? If you can see any veins in your arms check the colour. See, blue.

And the truth is...

Your blood is red, as you will have noticed anytime you have cut yourself. Don't do this on purpose just to check because:

1. ***You might die***
2. ***It'll make a mess***
3. ***It will hurt***
4. ***You might die. We know this is the same as point 1, but it's such a good point it's worth making twice.***

Blood gets its colour from a mixture of something called haemoglobin, iron and oxygen. The more oxygen that is mixed with the blood, the redder it looks – but at no point will it look blue. The veins only look blue because of the way our skin absorbs light, which bounces back more blue light than any other colour.

So all blood is red – even the Queen's. Sorry Ma'am.

Verdict: BUSTED

Raindrops are shaped like teardrops

You will have seen it countless times; raindrops hanging from your umbrella, or dangling off the window ledges. You want to be outside, but you can't be because it's raining. Wet weather can be so depressing even the raindrops look like tears.

★ And the truth is...

What you are looking at are drips, not drops. Raindrops come in a couple of basic shapes depending on their size. Small raindrops are actually round – or to be precise, they're spherical. This is because the surface tension of the water keeps it that shape. Raindrops bigger than 1mm across are a more complicated shape, a bit like a deflated football. That's because the pressure of the air under the raindrop is flattening the bottom slightly, and altering the drop's shape.

So two shapes and neither of them look like teardrops.

Verdict: BUSTED

KILLER SCIENCE

The scientists that died for their work - literally

Alexander Bogdanov (1873-1928)

Blood transfusion is the process where blood is pumped into a body to replace blood that has been lost. Without transfusions many operations would be impossible and many, many people would die. As a result adults are encouraged to donate blood so it can be used in hospitals.

Alexander Bogdanov was a Russian scientist who pioneered blood transfusions. He was such a fan that he used them on himself – not to keep him alive, but because he thought it kept him young and healthy. Unfortunately for him he got this last bit a little wrong.

These days donated blood is carefully checked to make sure it is free from disease. Bogdanov didn't think of this and accidently ended up injecting himself with infected blood. He died as a result.

Alfred Nobel

Alfred Nobel was a Swedish inventor who is now most famous for the prestigious awards named after him – the Nobel Prizes. However, it was his work in the construction industry that brought his fame and wealth.

Nobel found a way of using nitroglycerine – a powerful explosive but so unstable it would blow up if not treated with the most delicate care. Nobel's success was to find a way of making nitroglycerine stable, but to keep its explosive power. He called his new invention dynamite.

Soon Nobel's companies were blasting their way to riches making canals, or mining, or in any other project that needed things blowing up. Unfortunately for the peace-loving Nobel, this also meant blowing people up. Governments across the globe were not slow in using Nobel's invention to make more powerful weapons than ever before.

Noble's biggest blunder was not to realise that other people were not as peace-loving as he was.

From way back in history, people noticed that moving from the shade into sunlight could make you sneeze. Even the famous Ancient Greek scientist Aristotle wrote about it. Does this mean people can be allergic to the Sun?

And the truth is...

About one third of the population suffer from what scientists call the photic sneeze reflex. Curiously, no one can say exactly why it happens as no proper studies have been done. Scientists guess that it might have something to do with messages from the eyes getting misinterpreted by the brain. The eyes close slightly in reaction to the sunlight, the brain thinks the nose is irritated, so the person sneezes.

Whatever the reason, wearing sunglasses solves the problem.

Flesh-eating plants can feed on mammals

Plants – we eat them, feed them to animals or dig them up because we think they're weeds. Not surprising then that the idea of plants getting their revenge and gobbling us up has been a much-used idea in books and films. Although the chances of getting chased down the street by a ferocious dandelion is non-existent; not everything is safe.

And the truth is...

Carnivorous plants do exist, take the insect eating Venus Flytrap or the sundew for example. Pitcher plants are like living jugs, partly filled with a watery liquid. Animals are attracted to the liquid, then fall in and slowly dissolve – and this is where the plant finds the nutrients which it needs to grow. The larger varieties, such as *Nepenthes attenboroughii* from the Philippines, are big enough to trap snakes, birds and even small mammals such as rats. Yummy.

Verdict: 

Gripes about Gravity

We've already seen how sci-fi films put the fiction into science (see page 27) so it won't come as much as surprise that there's even more stuff that they get wrong. And if there's a movie that features an alien planet then the chances are it's made a grave mistake about gravity.

We've all seen the footage of the astronauts on the Moon doing that funny bouncy walk thing. As you will have read on page 44, it's because the Moon has less gravity. However, no matter which planet our movie stars end up on they always get to walk around like they're on Earth – no matter how big or small the new planet is – the gravity is always the same!

It's often said that big movie stars need to stay real and keep their feet on the ground – well in sci-fi films they do just that!

Human beings have five senses

Your senses are your way of knowing where you are and what you are doing. Your five senses are: sight, smell, hearing, taste and touch. The brain receives the information from your senses in the form of electrical impulses which your nerves send when they detect something. These are all your brain needs to know what's going on and how to react to any given situation.

And the truth is...

Scientists today believe that you might have anywhere between nine and twenty-one senses. These include the ability to feel pain, pressure, temperature and where your limbs are in relation to your own body. You can try this last one very easily: close your eyes and lift your arm up. You know exactly where your arm is, but you're not looking at it and it's not touching anything or being touched.

It seems we need more than five senses after all.

Verdict: BUSTED

Ptolemy

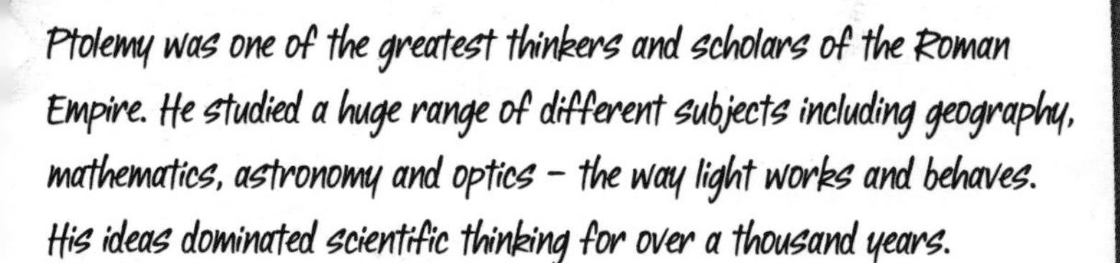

Ptolemy was one of the greatest thinkers and scholars of the Roman Empire. He studied a huge range of different subjects including geography, mathematics, astronomy and optics – the way light works and behaves. His ideas dominated scientific thinking for over a thousand years.

He knew that the Earth was a sphere and calculated the size of it. He suggested the idea of splitting the globe into lines of latitude and longitude to make navigation easier – a system we have today. He also described the way the planets move.

Unfortunately he got two fairly major points totally wrong. Firstly he thought the Sun and planets orbited around Earth. Secondly his calculations on the size of the Earth made it smaller than it really was. Fourteen hundred years later Columbus would land in the West Indies thinking it was India – and it was all thanks to Ptolemy and his dodgy maths.

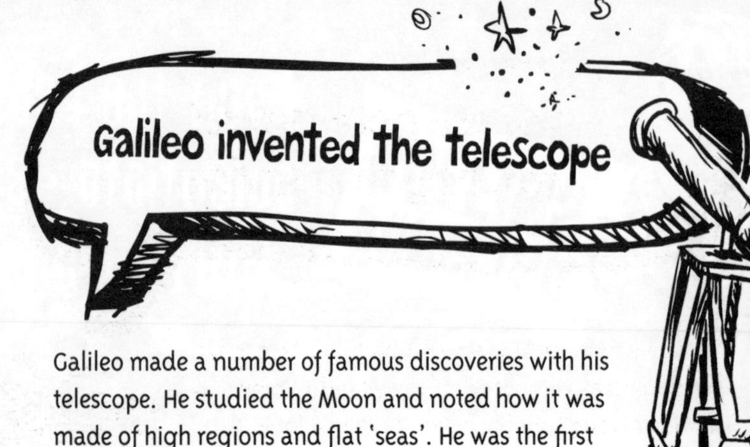

Galileo made a number of famous discoveries with his telescope. He studied the Moon and noted how it was made of high regions and flat 'seas'. He was the first person to see some of the moons around Jupiter. He also studied Venus and even the Sun. Almost as remarkable as his discoveries is the fact that he made his telescope himself.

And the truth is...

Although Galileo did make his own telescope, he wasn't the first person to do so. It's unclear where the idea originated, but historians think it may have been a German-Dutch man called Hans Lippershey, who made the first ones in 1608.

Galileo made his own versions, but being the clever so-and-so that he was he did it without actually seeing what one of the existing telescopes looked like. He simply heard about what a telescope could do and figured out how it worked. And by all accounts Galileo's telescopes were the best in the world at the time. Galileo had taken that most important second step – he had taken an invention and improved on it.

Verdict: BUSTED

You use more muscles frowning than smiling

You have muscles all over your body – which is a good thing as without them you wouldn't move. However, you probably have a heck of a lot more of them than you think. For example, did you know that you have 43 muscles in just your face? This might seem a lot but think about all the many little movements you can make: eyebrows raising, eyelids shutting, nostrils flaring, mouth opening and closing and so on and so on. All these movements rely on more than one muscle, and that's true for smiling as well as frowning.

And the truth is:

You use twelve facial muscles to make a genuine smile and eleven to pull a frown. This might make it sound like it takes less effort to look grumpy, but it seems that the muscles you use to smile are used more often than the frowning muscles so are more used to doing the work. In short, smiling is easier, but uses more muscle.

Verdict: BUSTED

Objects sink because they are heavier than water

Throw a feather in a river and what does it do? It floats of course. Now try it with a stone. It sinks like ... well, a stone. The feather is light so it floats; the stone sinks because it's heavy. Job done, what's next?

And the truth is...

But hold on a minute, what are big ships made from? Why metal of course. So how do *they* float?

The answer is air. A ship covers a big area with a little bit of metal with lots of air inside it. The combined weight of metal and air is less than the water it sits on, so the ship stays afloat.

So objects sink because they are heavier than water – but heavier than water objects can be made to float!

WEIRD WEATHER

Dusty Disasters

A dust storm, or haboob as it is also known, is when strong winds carry loose material such as dry soil in a low lying cloud. Dust storms are bad news; apart form the damage they can cause to the areas that they pass over, there is also the loss of valuable top soil from the area the dust storm occurred.

Dust storms can be huge. For example, a dust storm hit the Phoenix area in Arizona, USA, in October 2011. The storm was figured to be around 80 km (50 miles) wide, 800m (half a mile) high and travelling at 64 km/h (40 mph).

Storms like these occur quite frequently during the summer months and can also be seen over sandy deserts – they are known as sand storms, of course.

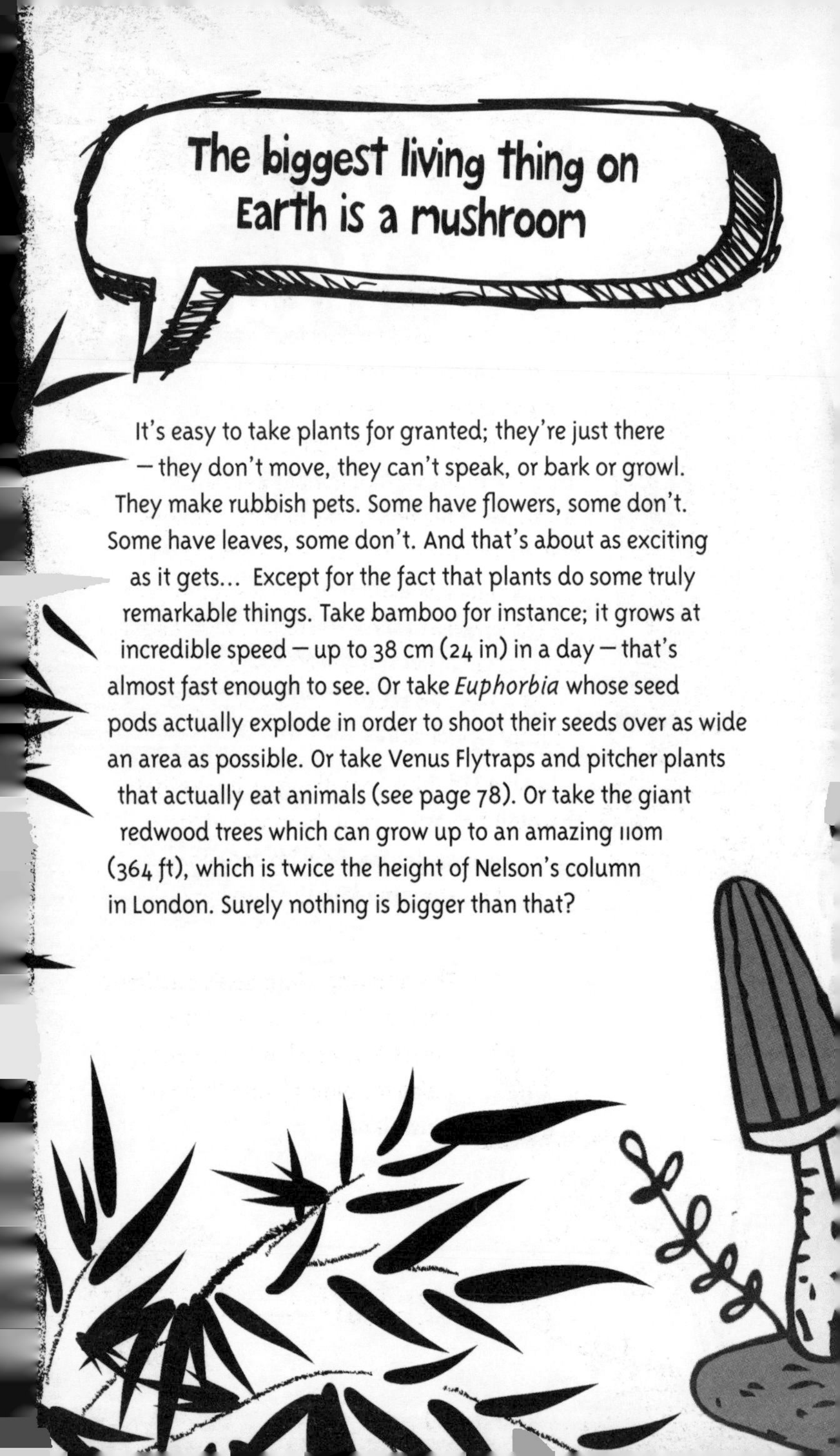

The biggest living thing on Earth is a mushroom

It's easy to take plants for granted; they're just there – they don't move, they can't speak, or bark or growl. They make rubbish pets. Some have flowers, some don't. Some have leaves, some don't. And that's about as exciting as it gets... Except for the fact that plants do some truly remarkable things. Take bamboo for instance; it grows at incredible speed – up to 38 cm (24 in) in a day – that's almost fast enough to see. Or take *Euphorbia* whose seed pods actually explode in order to shoot their seeds over as wide an area as possible. Or take Venus Flytraps and pitcher plants that actually eat animals (see page 78). Or take the giant redwood trees which can grow up to an amazing 110m (364 ft), which is twice the height of Nelson's column in London. Surely nothing is bigger than that?

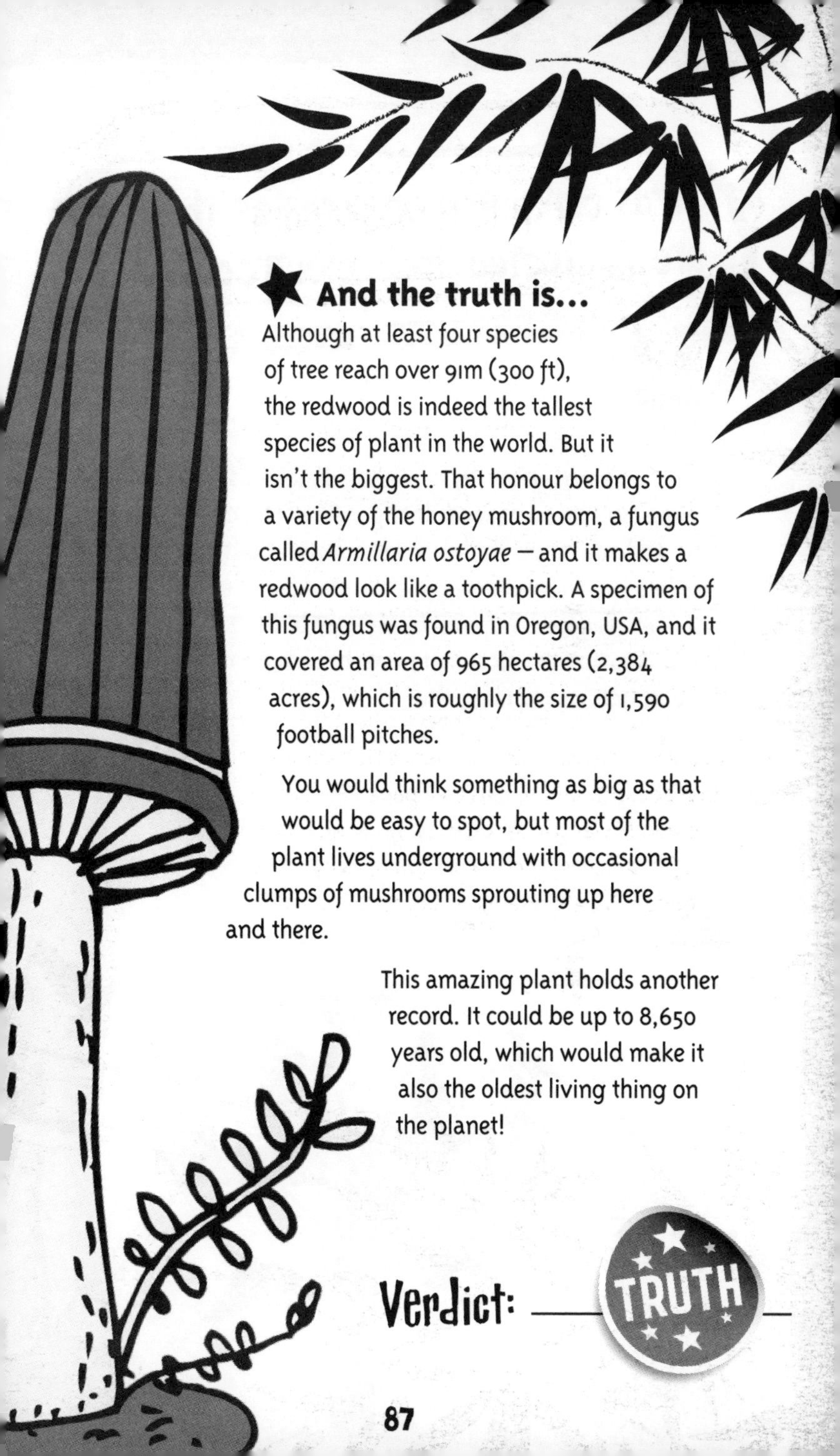

And the truth is...

Although at least four species of tree reach over 91m (300 ft), the redwood is indeed the tallest species of plant in the world. But it isn't the biggest. That honour belongs to a variety of the honey mushroom, a fungus called *Armillaria ostoyae* – and it makes a redwood look like a toothpick. A specimen of this fungus was found in Oregon, USA, and it covered an area of 965 hectares (2,384 acres), which is roughly the size of 1,590 football pitches.

You would think something as big as that would be easy to spot, but most of the plant lives underground with occasional clumps of mushrooms sprouting up here and there.

This amazing plant holds another record. It could be up to 8,650 years old, which would make it also the oldest living thing on the planet!

Verdict: TRUTH

Birds can perch on wires as they are 'protected' from electrocution

We all know that electricity cables are dangerous. You don't go messing around near electricity pylons – touch one of those wires and you might not live to tell anyone about how stupid you've been. So how come birds can stand on the wires and not suffer any ill-effects? It must be because birds have some kind of insulation on their feet that protects them from the electric current. Or is it something else?

And the truth is...

The answer lies in how electricity travels. Electricity needs a start and end point and something to travel on from one to the other. This is called a circuit. Electricity also likes to take the easiest path, which is important for the birds, as is the fact that some substances conduct electricity better than other materials. When birds sit on a wire the electricity continues on its path, because the wire conducts electricity better than birds do. However if the bird had one foot on the wire and one on something else – like the pole for example – then the bird would make a new circuit, the electricity would flow through the bird and the bird would get frazzled.

A penny dropped from a tall building will kill someone

There are various versions of this story, involving the Empire State Building or the Eiffel Tower, but the general theme is the same – if you drop a small coin from a very tall building you could kill someone. The idea is that a coin falling from a great height will pick up so much speed it will be travelling as fast as a bullet. So don't drop coins out of a high window or you could be up on a murder charge.

And the truth is...

Objects don't keep speeding up as they fall, instead they reach 'terminal velocity', the fastest speed gravity will pull them to Earth. A penny's terminal velocity is about 2.4m/sec (8.8 ft/ sec), BUT – and as you can see it's a big but – pennies do not fly through the air well. Their shape is not aerodynamic, so they flutter and spin through the air which slows them down. Also the air around big buildings is gusty which would slow the penny down further.

By the time the penny reaches the ground,
the worst it is likely to do is give
somebody a bruise.
Verdict:
BUSTED

You need to drink eight glasses of water a day

Around 60% of the human body is made of water, so keeping our liquid intake high is necessary for our survival. Humans need water more than they need food. You could go over 70 days without food before starving to death, but you wouldn't last more than 14 days without water.

When your body runs low on liquid you become what is called dehydrated. Feeling thirsty is a good sign that you need to take more liquids on board. It has become an accepted fact that you need to drink around eight glasses of water a day to stay healthy.

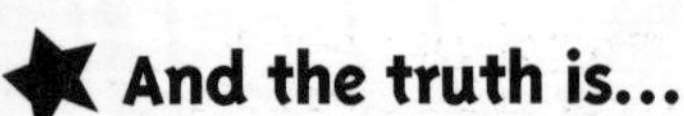

And the truth is...

While the amount of liquid you need each day might be about right, the way to take it isn't. Your body needs liquid, which doesn't mean just water. It can come from all sorts of sources: tea, milk, and importantly, food. Besides, a large man is going to need more liquid than a small child, so you have to be careful with general advice like this.

Verdict: BUSTED

All planets are rocky and pockmarked with craters

There's a lot of rock out there in space. Apart from our own lovely planet there are other planets, moons, asteroids and meteoroids. With all that stuff floating about there is bound to be the occasional accident. Take a look at the moon through a pair of binoculars and you'll see the result of some of these collisions – huge craters caused when meteorites have hit the surface.

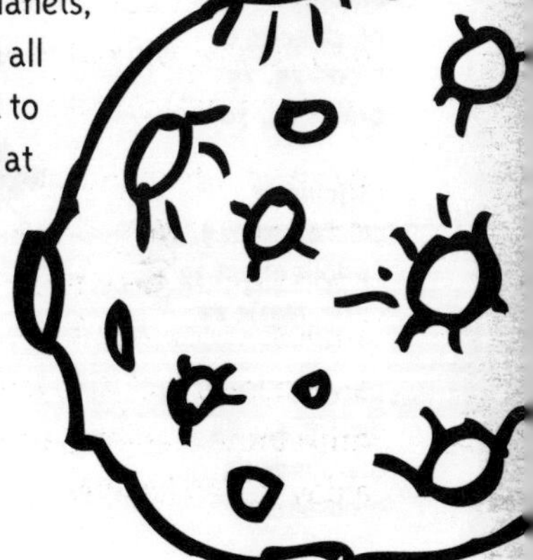

★ And the truth is...

There is a lot of rock out there, but not everything is rocky. The bigger planets are actually made of gas – half the planets in our solar system are like this. Also, the craters happen most frequently on planets and moons without an atmosphere. Earth has an atmosphere so most meteorites burn up in the air. The Moon doesn't so it gets hit every time.

So if a planet is made of gas or has an atmosphere it's not going to be rocky or pockmarked.

Verdict: BUSTED

Where can I find myths about...

100%

SUCKER-PROOF

GUARANTEED!

Take a look at our other marvellously mythbusting titles...

Tip: Turn over!